THE DANIEL PLAN ESSENTIALS SERIES

FOOD

FOOD

Essential Two

ENJOYING GOD'S ABUNDANCE

STUDY GUIDE

FOUR SESSIONS

featuring

DR. MARK HYMAN
& DEE EASTMAN
with KAREN LEE-THORP

ZONDERVAN

Food Study Guide

This title is also available as a Zondervan ebook. Visit www.zondervan.com/ebooks.

Requests for information should be addressed to:
Zondervan, *3900 Sparks Dr. SE, Grand Rapids, Michigan 49546*

ISBN 978-0-310-81999-8

Cover photography: iStockphoto
Interior photography: Robert Ortiz, Kent Cameron, Don Haynes, Robert Hawkins, Shelly Antol, Matt Armendariz, the PICS Ministry at Saddleback Church, iStockphoto, 123rf.com
Interior design: Kait Lamphere

First Printing May 2015 / Printed in the United States of America

Contents

Welcome Letter

I am so glad you have joined us for this Daniel Plan study. I am excited for your journey, as I have seen firsthand that change is within reach as you embrace the Daniel Plan lifestyle. This groundbreaking program will equip you with practical tools to bring health into every area of your life. It has been transformative for thousands of people around the world and can be for you as well.

I speak from experience. I've not only witnessed endless stories of life change but have personally benefited from these Daniel Plan Essentials for many years now. Working full-time with five grown children, including identical triplet girls, I understand what it is like to juggle many priorities and have my health impacted. The key elements of The Daniel Plan have been completely restorative in my life as I have integrated them one step at a time.

As you go through this four-week study, the perfect complement to maximize your success is reading *The Daniel Plan: 40 Days to a Healthier Life*. The book includes a 40-day food and fitness guide, complete with a meal plan, recipes, shopping lists, and exercises that will energize your efforts. It will complement any of The Daniel Plan studies you dive into. There are also numerous articles and free resources on our website (www.danielplan.com), along with a weekly newsletter filled with tools and inspiration to keep you flourishing.

Congratulations on taking the next step to gaining vitality in your life. My prayer is that you will be inspired and fully equipped to continue your journey, and that you will experience a whole new level of wellness in the process. I pray that you will feel God's presence and will be reenergized to follow all he has planned for you.

For His Glory,

Dee Eastman

Dee Eastman
Founding Director, The Daniel Plan

How to Use This Guide

There are five video studies in The Daniel Plan series, one for each of the five Essentials (Faith, Food, Fitness, Focus, and Friends). Each study is four sessions long. The studies may be done in any order. If your group is new, consider starting with the six-week *The Daniel Plan Study Guide* and companion DVD, which offers an overview of all five Essentials.

GROUP SIZE

Each Daniel Plan video study is designed to be experienced in a group setting such as a Bible study, Sunday school class, or any small group gathering. To ensure that everyone has enough time to participate in discussions, it is recommended that large groups break into smaller groups of four to six people each.

MATERIALS NEEDED

Each participant should have his or her own study guide, which includes notes for video segments, directions for activities, discussion questions, and ideas for personal application between sessions. This curriculum is best used in conjunction with *The Daniel Plan: 40 Days to a Healthier Life*, which includes a complete 40-day food and fitness guide that complements this study.

TIMING

Each session is designed to be completed in 60 to 90 minutes, depending on your setting and the size of your group. Each video is approximately 20 minutes long.

OUTLINE OF EACH SESSION

Each group session will include the following:

- *Coming Together.* The foundation for spiritual growth is an intimate connection with God and his family. A few people who really know you and earn your trust provide a place to experience the life Jesus invites you to live. This opening portion of your meeting is an opportunity to transition from your busy life into your group time.

  In Session 1 you'll find some icebreaker questions on the session topic, along with guidelines that state the values your group will live by so that everyone feels comfortable sharing. In Sessions 2–4 you'll have a chance to check in with other group members to report praise and progress toward your goals of healthy living. You'll also be able to share how you chose to put the previous session's insights into practice—and what the results were. There's no pressure for everyone to answer. This is time to get to know each other better and cheer each other on.

- *Learning Together.* This is the time when you will view the video teaching segment. This study guide provides notes on the key points of the video teaching along with space for you to write additional thoughts and questions.

- *Growing Together.* Here is where you will discuss the teaching you watched. The focus will be on how the teaching intersects with your real life.

- *What I Want to Remember.* You'll have a couple of minutes after your discussion to write down one or two key insights from the teaching and discussion that you want to remember.

- *Better Together.* The Daniel Plan is all about transforming the way you actually live. So before you close your meeting in prayer, you'll take some time to think about how you might apply what you've discussed. Under "Next Steps" you'll find a list of things you can do to put the session's insights into practice. Then the "Food Tip of the Week" offers a bonus video with a great recipe or food idea. It is on your DVD if you want to view it together with your group. It is also available online for you to view on your own during the week. Likewise, the "Fitness Move of the Week" is a bonus video with a simple exercise you can add to your fitness practices. It, too, is on your DVD and online.

Encourage each other to be specific about one or two things you plan to do each week as next steps. Consider asking someone in the group to be your buddy to hold each other accountable. Create an atmosphere of fun and positive reinforcement.

» *Praying Together.* The group session will close with time for a response to God in prayer, thanking him for what he's doing for you and asking for his help to live out what you have learned. Ideas for group prayer, as well as a written closing prayer, are provided. Feel free to use them or not. Consider having different group members lead the prayer time.

Learning to Live Abundantly

"I have learned how to be content with whatever I have."
Philippians 4:11 (NLT)

God has made so many delicious and nutrient-rich foods for us to enjoy. Bell peppers and blueberries, eggs, carrots, cucumbers—we have an overflowing variety of foods available to us at our local grocery store, more than at any time in the history of the world. And although we need to learn to make choices, eating well doesn't have to be as complicated as it may seem. By choosing real foods and avoiding processed and refined products, we begin to experience the healing that good nutrition provides.

In this study on Food, we'll learn how to make those good choices to boost our energy, maximize our metabolism, and revitalize our health. We'll begin in this session by looking at a simple method of meal planning: the Daniel Plan Plate.

COMING TOGETHER

If this is your first time meeting together as a group, take a moment to introduce yourself.

Also, pass around a sheet of paper on which each person can write his or her name, address, phone number, and email address. Ask for a volunteer to type up the list and email it to everyone else this week.

Finally, you'll need some simple group guidelines that outline values and expectations. See the sample in the Appendix and make sure that everyone agrees with and understands those expectations.

When you're finished with these introductory activities, give everyone a chance to respond to these icebreaker questions:

» Describe a typical day of eating when you were ten years old. What did you eat? What were a few favorite foods?

» In one word, how would you summarize what food represented to you when you were ten? For example: *comfort, pleasure, worry, reward, celebration, necessity, boredom.*

LEARNING TOGETHER

AN INTERVIEW WITH Dr. Mark Hyman

Play the video segment for Session 1. As you watch, use the outline provided to follow along or to take additional notes on anything that stands out to you.

» To live abundantly, we want to leave the food that man made and eat the food that God made. If it was made in a plant, don't eat it. If it was grown on a plant, eat it.

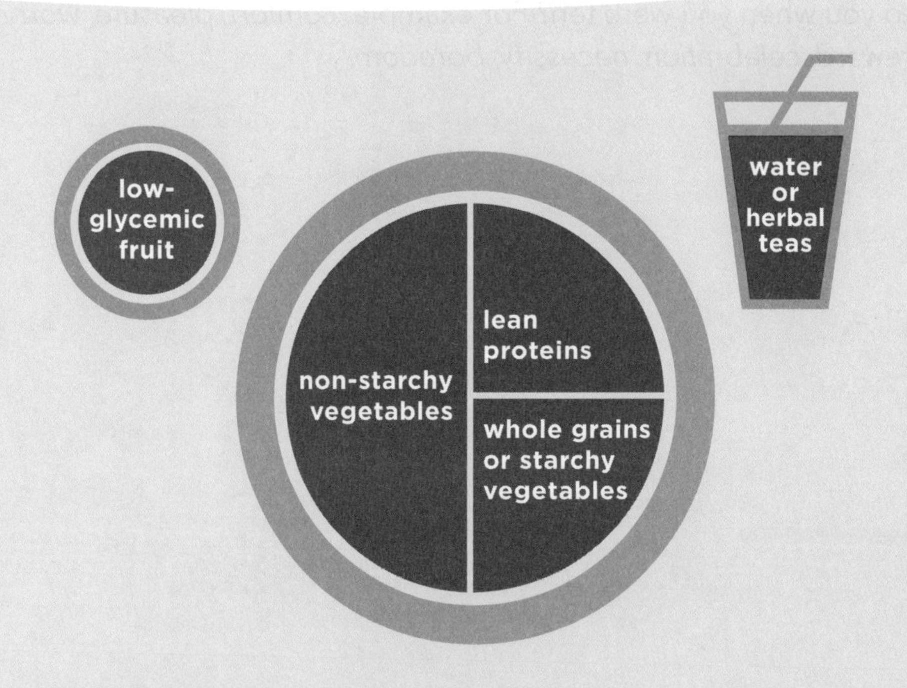

» Many people's palates have been hijacked by the food industry.

» If you feel lousy, it might be related to what you're eating. The Daniel Plan is about giving you the opportunity to serve God better by feeling good. If you eat good, you feel good, and you can do good.

» The Daniel Plan Plate for any meal contains:
  - 50 percent non-starchy veggies
  - 25 percent healthy animal or vegetable proteins
  - 25 percent healthy starch or whole grains
  - Side of low-glycemic fruit
  - Drink – water or herbal teas

TOP 10 CHOICES IN EACH FOOD GROUP to Get You Started

NON-STARCHY VEGGIES	PROTEIN	STARCH OR GRAIN	LOW-GLYCEMIC FRUIT
Asparagus	Beans	Beets	Apples
Bell peppers	Beef	Brown or black rice	Blackberries
Broccoli	Chicken	Buckwheat	Blueberries
Cauliflower	Eggs	Carrots	Gogi berries
Collard greens	Halibut	Corn	Grapefruit
Cucumbers	Lentils	Green peas	Kiwi
Green beans	Nuts	Quinoa	Nectarines
Kale	Salmon	Sweet potatoes	Peaches
Spinach	Seeds	Turnips	Plums
Zucchini	Turkey	Winter squash	Raspberries

» The Daniel Plan encourages you to eat as much as you want of non-starchy vegetables. They are filled with phytonutrients, plant chemicals that heal your body. They also have vitamins, minerals, and fiber.

» Healthy animal or vegetable proteins are ones without hormones, antibiotics, heavy metals, and chemicals. Organic and grass-fed animal proteins are good choices.

» Healthy starches do not include white flour because your body metabolizes flour like sugar. Flour and sugar contribute to obesity and diabetes.

» There are many simple ways to include more vegetables in your diet. Here are several:

- *Cauliflower made like mashed potatoes.* Boil a whole cauliflower for about ten minutes. Mash it with ¼ cup of the cooking liquid, a little butter or coconut oil, garlic, and salt.
- *Steamed broccoli.* Steam broccoli heads and drizzle them with lemon and olive oil.
- *Stir-fried greens.* Stir-fry greens in olive oil with chopped ginger and salt.
- *Roasted mushrooms.* Drizzle raw mushrooms with olive oil on a cookie sheet. Add garlic and salt. Roast in the oven until they are soft, about twenty minutes at 350 degrees.
- *Dips.* Dip raw vegetables in fresh guacamole, fresh salsa, or hummus.

» For fruits, aim for darkly colored low-sugar fruits. Avoid high-sugar fruits like pineapple and grapes.

» What you eat matters. The right foods turn on genes, improve your hormones, balance the way proteins function in your body, strengthen your immune system, and keep your gut bacteria healthy.

» Sugar is the biggest driver of obesity, heart disease, diabetes, and cancer. It also drives dementia, depression, acne, and infertility.

» Diabesity (a spectrum of health problems from pre-diabetes to type II diabetes) means that your blood sugar is out of balance and you are storing belly fat. It affects one out of every two Americans. The way to fight it is to pay attention to the *glycemic load* of the food, which is how fast it raises your blood sugar.

» Good fats don't make you fat. Eating some fat is essential for your brain to function and for your cells to be built. Hormones are made from cholesterol. Good fats include olive oil, nuts, seeds, coconut, and omega-3 fats from fish. Even moderate amounts of animal fat are not that bad.

» Sugar increases belly fat, makes your metabolism slow down, and actually makes you hungry.

» Sugary drinks like sweetened coffees, sodas, and even fruit juice are a major source of problem sugar. Instead of these, we should drink water. Water can be flavored with lemon or a little cranberry or pomegranate juice. Sparkling water is fine.

Note: Chapter 10 of *The Daniel Plan* book contains a 40-day core meal plan, complete with recipes and shopping lists. The Appendix of this study guide contains five days of the meal plan, along with recipes and a shopping list, to get you started.

GROWING TOGETHER

Discuss what you learned from the video. Don't feel obliged to answer every question. Select those that most resonate with your group.

What did you hear in the video that had the most impact on you?

"Do you not know that your bodies are temples of the Holy Spirit, who is in you, whom you have received from God? You are not your own; you were bought at a price. Therefore honor God with your bodies."

1 Corinthians 6:19–20

What motivates you to change the way you have been eating? (For example: symptoms of pre-diabetes, the desire to feel better so that you can do more good in the world, or the awareness that your body is a temple of the Holy Spirit.)

Which of Dr. Hyman's recommendations listed below can you imagine starting to follow this week? (Remember: small steps lead to big results.) Which ones seem like more of a reach for you? Why?

- Eating more non-starchy vegetables in recipes like those described in the Notes

- Eating healthy proteins – no more than 25 percent of your plate at each meal

- Making starchy vegetables and whole grains 25 percent of your plate at each meal

- Choosing low-sugar fruits

- Drinking water instead of sugary drinks like sweetened coffees, soda, and fruit juice

- Minimizing foods made with flour, like bread and pasta

- Eating good fats, like olive oil, nuts, seeds, coconut oil, and omega-3 fats from fish

"I can do everything through Christ, who gives me strength."

Philippians 4:13 (NLT)

What questions do you have about anything in the video?

5 What resistance (fears, concerns) do you have to the way of eating that Dr. Hyman recommends? What would help you address those concerns?

6 In the Appendix, look over the 5-day sample meal plan and the recipes that follow it. What is your reaction to trying out this meal plan? (You can find the full 40-day meal plan in *The Daniel Plan* book.)

7 What support can this group give you as you experiment with this new way of eating? For example, do you want a buddy to go shopping with? Do you want to make some of the recipes together and then let each family take part of the food home?

What I Want
to Remember

Complete this activity on your own.

» Briefly review the video outline and any notes you took. Review also any notes from the discussion.

» In the space below, write down the most significant thing you gained from this session—from the video or the discussion. You can share it with the group if you wish.

BETTER TOGETHER

Now that you've talked about some great ideas, let's get practical – and put what you're learning into action. The Daniel Plan centers around five essential areas of health. In this study you're exploring Food, so you can begin by identifying one or two steps you can take to enjoy God's abundance of healthy food. Then check out the Food Tip of the Week and the Fitness Move of the Week for some fresh ideas to enrich your journey toward health in those areas. There are also many tips and tools on the danielplan.com website so you can keep growing in all of the Essentials while doing this study. Use or adapt whatever is helpful to you!

FOOD

Next Steps

Here are a few suggested activities to help you take your first steps in eating according to The Daniel Plan. Check one or two boxes next to the options you'd like to try this week – choose what works for you.

☐ Follow the 5-day sample of the 40-day meal plan. Take your shopping list to the grocery store and buy what you need for those first five days. Then dive in!

☐ Add more veggies to your meals this week. Try some of the recipes suggested in this session or others you know of. *The Daniel Plan* book and *The Daniel Plan Cookbook* have more ideas for enjoying veggies.

☐ Team up with one or more members of your group to go shopping for veggies, low-sugar fruits, whole grains (not flour products), and healthy proteins.

☐ Team up with one or more group members to cook recipes from the 5-day meal plan or other healthy recipes.

☐ Stock your refrigerator with healthy foods for a family on the go, as described in the Food Tip of the Week.

- ☐ Say no to sugary drinks like soda, fruit juice, and sweetened coffee. Say yes to plenty of water or herbal teas.

- ☐ Have a family conference where you talk about trying The Daniel Plan meal plan for a month.

- ☐ Get *The Daniel Plan* book to investigate the full 40-day core meal plan.

- ☐ Get *The Daniel Plan Cookbook* to see more recipes.

- ☐ Memorize one verse related to Food. See the memory verses in the Appendix.

Food Tip
of the Week

Whether you have a family of one, two, four, or more, this week's food tip is full of great suggestions for healthy foods that you can "grab and go" out the door with to make easy healthy eating on the run. Just click the Food Tip of the Week on your video screen (3 minutes), scan the QR code, or go to danielplan.com/foodtip.

Fitness Move
of the Week

Check out this great stretch for your lower back, hamstrings, and glutes. It will fuel your body by getting blood circulating. Just click the Fitness Move of the Week on your video screen (1 minute), use the QR code, or go to danielplan.com/fitnessmove.

Praying *Together*

Because everything we do in our journey toward health depends on God's power, we end each meeting with prayer and encourage group members to pray for each other during the week.

"If you sinful people know how to give good gifts to your children, how much more will your heavenly Father give the Holy Spirit to those who ask him."
Luke 11:13 (NLT)

This week, ask your heavenly Father to give you power from the Holy Spirit to care for your bodies, which are temples of the Holy Spirit. Ask him for power from the Holy Spirit to choose healthy food. Give group members a chance to offer up one- or two-sentence prayers asking for the Holy Spirit's help in the areas of eating that will be new for them. Our habits of eating are deeply rooted, and we need God's strength to change them.

Have someone close with this prayer:

Thank you, Lord, for giving us guidance about how we should eat in order to care for our bodies so that we can serve you. Thank you that you love us too much to leave us in our unhealthy habits. Please fill us with your Holy Spirit, so that we can make changes and experiment with new things. Please change our palates so that we can enjoy the rich flavors of the fruits and vegetables and whole grains you created. Please show us how we can encourage and support each other in healthy eating. Thank you for this group. I pray this in Jesus' name. Amen.

Jumpstart Your Health

"Food for the stomach and the stomach for food, and God will destroy them both."
1 Corinthians 6:13

Gradual, step-by-step changes to your diet can make a big difference over time if you keep at them. However, if you feel lousy because of what you have been eating, it can be helpful to take some big steps for just ten days to detoxify your body from the unhealthy foods it has been dependent on. In this session we will look at the foods that trigger health problems in many people, and we'll suggest a detox plan to eliminate those foods for a period of time so that your body can take a giant leap forward in feeling better.

Leader: During your group discussion in this session, you will practice reading the labels on packaged foods to look for problem ingredients. Plan ahead to bring at least a dozen items for the group to examine. Possibilities include cooking oil, shortening, margarine, salad dressings, ketchup, mayonnaise, cookies, chips, snacks, and many others—anything with an ingredient list on the package. If you're meeting in a home, the host can supply these items. See questions 3 and 5.

COMING TOGETHER

The other members of your group can be a huge source of support in sustaining healthy changes in your life. Before watching the video, check in with each other about your experiences since the last session. For example:

» Briefly share what Next Steps from Session 1 you completed or tried to complete. How did it go? What went well? Do you have any questions after trying the steps? What encouragement do you need?

» How did Session 1 affect the way you think about food or your body?

» Have you been practicing The Daniel Plan in other areas, such as Fitness? If so, what have you done? What is working well for you? What questions do you have? What encouragement do you need?

LEARNING TOGETHER

AN INTERVIEW WITH **Dr. Mark Hyman**

Play the video segment for Session 2. As you watch, use the outline provided to follow along or to take additional notes on anything that stands out to you.

» A 10-day detox can make dramatic changes in how you feel. It can lower blood sugar and blood pressure, as well as reduce symptoms of migraines, irritable bowel, depression, acne, eczema, joint pain, fatigue, and insomnia.

» The 10-day detox is ten days of avoiding all of the foods that commonly trigger health problems in people. It restarts your metabolism, taste buds, brain chemistry, and hormones. After ten days, you can decide to add foods back to your diet, one at a time, to see how each individual food affects how you feel.

» The first harmful product that we need to eliminate is the bad forms of fat, the processed fats. Most forms of fat are fine to eat if they are in their natural state. Bad fats include processed and refined vegetable oils like corn oil, soy oil, canola oil, or products labeled just "vegetable oil." We need to replace them with unrefined oils like grape seed oil and extra-virgin olive oil. Good, unrefined oils often say *cold-pressed* or *expeller-pressed* on the label.

- The other bad type of fat is hydrogenated fat, also called trans fat. Shortening and margarine are examples of hydrogenated or trans fats. This type of fat causes diabetes and heart attacks. It's important to read the labels on products, and if you see the word *hydrogenated* on the ingredient list, don't eat the product. Throw it away.

- Next, we need to eliminate hidden sugar from our diet. Packaged breakfast cereals are all sugar. Salad dressings are made with sugar. Soft drinks and juice are sugar. Many pasta sauces are made with sugar. We need to think of sugar as a recreational drug, like alcohol, that has to be treated with great care.

» For the 10-day detox, we go off sugar 100 percent, because our bodies and brains are addicted to it. We need to break the addiction.

» We also go off all artificial sweeteners, because those also lead to obesity and diabetes. Whole-plant stevia can be okay once the detox is over.

» Next, we eliminate food additives. If you read the label on a product and it has an ingredient in Latin, something else you can't pronounce, or something you wouldn't put in a recipe, don't eat the product. This includes additives like maltodextrin, monosodium glutamate (MSG), and others. These are flavor enhancers and preservatives, and they are harmful. MSG stimulates appetite. It creates cravings. Likewise, yellow dye number 5 causes asthma and inflammation.

» If we get a sugar craving while on the detox, we need to have our pantries and refrigerators stocked with emergency foods to grab, such as nuts, apples, hard-boiled eggs, cut raw veggies and hummus, even strips of grilled chicken.

» To relieve the discomfort that comes during the first few days of detox while the body is breaking its addictions, it's important to drink plenty of water or herbal tea, take vitamin C and magnesium, and get plenty of fiber so that the body eliminates the toxins.

» There are two other types of food that we eliminate in the detox because many people are sensitive to them and get inflammation as a result. Those two foods are gluten and dairy products.

» Gluten is a protein in wheat, barley, rye, oats, and spelt. We avoid those grains for ten days to see if our bodies feel better without them. Then after ten days we try them again and see how our bodies react.

» Dairy products include butter, milk, and cheese—the products of cow's milk. Eggs are not dairy. We avoid dairy for ten days to see if our symptoms clear up.

GROWING TOGETHER

Discuss what you learned from the video. Don't feel obliged to answer every question. Select those that most resonate with your group.

1. What did you hear in the video that had the most impact on you?

2. How is 1 Corinthians 6:12 relevant to our food choices?

"'I have the right to do anything,' you say—but not everything is beneficial. 'I have the right to do anything'—but I will not be mastered by anything."
1 Corinthians 6:12

3. How can you tell the difference between good fats and bad fats? (If possible, let the group look at some bottled oils and evaluate them as refined or unrefined. On the labels, look for the words *cold-pressed* or *expeller-pressed*, which are often on the labels of good, unrefined oils. Also, if you have shortening or margarine available, look on the ingredient list for the word *hydrogenated*.)

What problems does sugar cause in our bodies? Do you think sugar could be a problem for you in the foods you eat? Why or why not?

5

Gather some products from your pantry and refrigerator: salad dressings, cookies and other baked goods, sauces, condiments, mayonnaise, and other products with labels. Read the ingredient list on each label, looking for sugar, any words you don't recognize, as well as the word *hydrogenated*. For more help with reading labels, view the Food Tip of the Week. Based on Dr. Hyman's recommendations, which of the products you have looked at should you not eat?

"So whether you eat or drink, or whatever you do, do it all for the glory of God."
1 Corinthians 10:31 (NLT)

Why does Dr. Hyman suggest going off dairy and gluten for ten days? What was your reaction to Dee's story about not knowing she was sensitive to gluten until she was off it for ten days and then ate it?

The 10-day detox is discussed in chapter 10 of *The Daniel Plan* book. It is similar to the 40-day core plan, but it cuts out dairy, gluten, and all sugars. What motivates you to try the detox? What resistance or concerns do you have? What would help to address your concerns?

The Lord is my strength and shield. I trust him with all my heart. He helps me, and my heart is filled with joy.
Psalm 28:7 (NLT)

What I Want *to Remember*

Complete this activity on your own.

- Briefly review the video outline and any notes you took. Review also any notes from the discussion.
- In the space below, write down the most significant thing you gained from this session—from the video or the discussion. You can share it with the group if you wish.

BETTER TOGETHER

Now that you've talked about some great ideas, let's get practical – and put what you're learning into action. Begin by identifying one or two steps you can take to live what you learned in this session. Then check out the Food Tip of the Week and the Fitness Move of the Week for some fresh ideas to enrich your journey toward health in those areas. Use or adapt whatever is helpful to you!

FOOD
Next Steps

Here are a few suggested activities to help you jumpstart your health. Check one or two boxes next to the options you'd like to try this week—choose what works for you.

- ☐ Clean out your pantry and refrigerator, ridding them of unhealthy items. Replace them with better alternatives. For guidelines, see "Cleaning Out Your Pantry" in the Appendix. The Food Tip of the Week for Session 4 can also help you know what to throw out and what to replace it with.

- ☐ Team up with a buddy to help each other clean out your pantries. Read the labels together to make good decisions about what to keep and what to toss.

- ☐ Do the 10-day detox in chapter 10 of *The Daniel Plan* book.

- ☐ Team up with a buddy to do the detox together. You can do your shopping together or just make contact during the week to encourage each other.

- ☐ Spend an hour at the beginning of the week to wash and chop vegetables and do whatever other prep you can do for the week's meals, so they'll be quick to prepare each day.

- ☐ Spend an hour making grab-and-go foods like vegetables and dip, hard-boiled eggs, and grilled chicken.

- ☐ Continue with the 40-day core meal plan in *The Daniel Plan* book.

- ☐ Memorize one verse related to Food. See the memory verses in the Appendix.

Food Tip
of the Week

Learning to read food labels is a crucial skill for making smart, healthy food choices. Become a food detective and uncover the bad ingredients to eliminate from your shopping cart. This week's food tip shows you how. Just click the Food Tip of the Week on your video screen (3 minutes), scan the QR code, or go to danielplan.com/foodtip.

Fitness Move
of the Week

This week's move teaches you to be conscious at every meal of how hungry or full you are. Just click the Fitness Move of the Week on your video screen (1 minute), use the QR code, or go to danielplan.com/fitnessmove.

Praying
Together

Because everything we do in our journey toward health depends on God's power, we end each meeting with prayer and encourage group members to pray for each other during the week.

"I can do everything through Christ, who gives me strength."
Philippians 4:13 (NLT)

This week, gather in smaller groups—two or three people each. Share with your partner(s) the prayer support you need in order to take your next step in The Daniel Plan. Do you need the faith and strength to start the 10-day detox? Are you feeling uncertain what to do? Do you want to thank God for the changes you have already begun to make? Pray for your partner(s). If you're new to praying in groups, it's fine to pray just a sentence or two.

Have someone close with this prayer:

Thank you, Lord, for showing us the foods that harm us. Please give us the wisdom and patience to reject those foods and choose other ones that will heal us. This is unfamiliar territory for some of us, and we need you to chart a path through it. Please fill us with your Holy Spirit for the power to follow through on the changes you want us to make. Show us how to support one another in this process. We want our eating to glorify you, and we know that we can do anything you call us to do through Christ, who gives us the strength. Thank you for walking with us on this journey. I pray this in Jesus' name. Amen.

CHROME PLATED

Cravings, Comfort Foods, and Choices

"He gives strength to the weary and increases the power of the weak."
Isaiah 40:29

Cravings. You know them well: those times when you just have to have something sweet, something salty, or something fried. In order for a food plan to work over the long term, it has to include a strategy for dealing with cravings. In this session you'll learn a strategy that works.

COMING TOGETHER

The other members of your group can be a huge source of support in sustaining healthy changes in your life. Before watching the video, check in with each other about your experiences since the last session. For example:

» Briefly share what Next Steps from Session 2 you completed or tried to complete. How did it go? What went well? Do you have any questions after trying the steps? What encouragement do you need?

» How did Session 2 affect the way you think about food or your body?

» Have you been practicing The Daniel Plan in other areas, such as Fitness? If so, what have you done? What is working well for you? What questions do you have? What encouragement do you need?

LEARNING TOGETHER

AN INTERVIEW WITH **Dr. Mark Hyman**

Play the video segment for Session 3. As you watch, use the outline provided to follow along or to take additional notes on anything that stands out to you.

» The Daniel Plan uses food as medicine to take back your brain chemistry, taste buds, and metabolism so you're not a victim of blood sugar and energy swings.

» To minimize cravings, mood swings, and energy swings:
- Eat every three to four hours.
- Have protein and fat for breakfast, not sugar or flour.
- Eat good, healthy fats.
- Cut way down on sugar and flour.

» Put a sign on the refrigerator that says, "What am I feeling? What do I need?"
- "I'm hungry and I need a snack."
- "I'm lonely and I need to talk to a friend."
- "I'm angry and I need to tell the person what I'm angry about so we can deal with this."
- "I'm sad and I need a hug and someone to hold me."
- "I'm exhausted and I need a nap."

- Make your home a safe zone where the foods at hand are healthy ones, and the unhealthy ones aren't there. For example, have dark chocolate (70 percent or higher) to dip into nut butter, and don't keep ice cream in the house.

- If you eat sugar, you will get a quick high and then crash. You will be hungry again, and you won't feel good.

- Create an emergency food pack that you keep with you. (See this week's Food Tip of the Week for ideas on what to pack.)

- Are you nourishing yourself by taking time for reflection, prayer, exercise, sleep, alone time, and time with friends? Do you need something to fill up your tank?

- Friends can nourish you. Encouragement from friends is a powerful antidote to cravings.

GROWING TOGETHER

Discuss what you learned from the video. Don't feel obliged to answer every question. Select those that most resonate with your group.

1. What foods do you tend to crave? What times of day do you tend to crave them?

2. What tactics from the video can you employ to deal with cravings at those times of day?

3. Which of the following feelings and needs masquerade as hunger in your life?

   » Loneliness—the need to talk to someone

   » Anger—the need to work through a conflict

   » Sadness—the need for a hug or time alone to cry or grieve

   » Exhaustion—the need for rest

What do you think might motivate a person to eat instead of dealing with loneliness, anger, sadness, or exhaustion directly?

5

How can those motivations be addressed in healthy ways? For example, how can other people be helpful?

6

Look at the "Top 10 Tips to Curb Your Cravings" in the Appendix. Read the first tip. What are the people, places, and things that trigger your cravings?

Read the following verses. How can they guide you when you feel too weak to resist cravings?

"We ourselves are like fragile clay jars containing this great treasure. This makes it clear that our great power is from God, not from ourselves."
2 Corinthians 4:7 (NLT)

"Each time [God] said, 'My grace is all you need. My power works best in weakness.' So now I am glad to boast about my weaknesses, so that the power of Christ can work through me."
2 Corinthians 12:9 (NLT)

What I Want *to Remember*

Complete this activity on your own.

» Briefly review the video outline and any notes you took. Review also any notes from the discussion.

» In the space below, write down the most significant thing you gained from this session—from the video or the discussion. You can share it with the group if you wish.

BETTER TOGETHER

Now that you've talked about some great ideas, let's get practical – and put what you're learning into action. Begin by identifying one or two steps you can take to live what you learned in this session. Then check out the Food Tip of the Week and the Fitness Move of the Week for some fresh ideas to enrich your journey toward health in those areas. Use or adapt whatever is helpful to you!

FOOD

Next Steps

Here are a few suggested activities to help you move forward in taming your cravings. Check one or two boxes next to the options you'd like to try this week – choose what works for you.

- ☐ Commit to eating breakfast every day this week with protein and fat, not sugar or flour.

- ☐ Stock your refrigerator and pantry with healthy snacks, and eliminate the unhealthy ones. Make your home a safe zone.

- ☐ Make a plan to cut way down on the sugar and flour you eat. What can you replace them with? Think about low-sugar fruits, whole grains, protein, and good fats like nuts. (If you're doing the detox, you're already off sugar and flour.)

- ☐ Pack an emergency food pack to keep with you. (See this week's Food Tip of the Week.) Take it to work to provide you with snacks. Keep it in your car if you're running errands. Take it to meetings, events at your children's school, and parties. Anyplace where you might get hungry or there might be refreshments served, make sure you have your healthy choices available.

- ☐ Put a sign on your refrigerator that says, "What am I feeling? What do I need?"

- [ ] Nourish yourself by taking time for reflection, prayer, exercise, sleep, alone time, or time with friends.

- [ ] Check in regularly with a buddy from your group to encourage each other to stick to The Daniel Plan. Talk about cravings and how you deal with them when they come up. Be accountable to each other for your choices. Even more important: be available if your buddy is lonely, sad, or angry and needs someone to talk to.

- [ ] Memorize a verse related to Food. See the memory verses in the Appendix.

Food Tip

of the Week

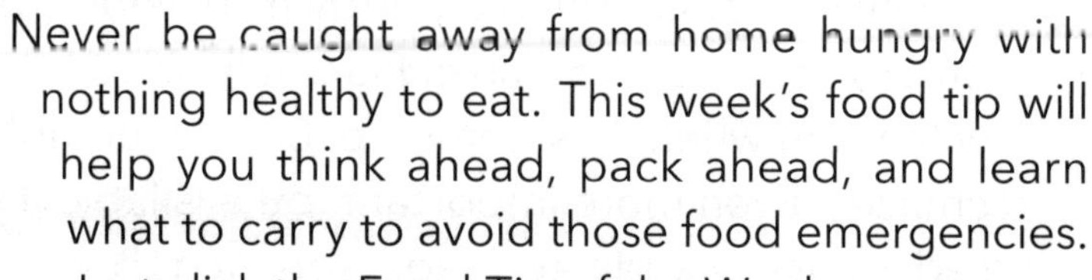

Never be caught away from home hungry with nothing healthy to eat. This week's food tip will help you think ahead, pack ahead, and learn what to carry to avoid those food emergencies. Just click the Food Tip of the Week on your video screen (3 minutes), scan the QR code, or go to danielplan.com/foodtip.

Fitness Move

of the Week

This week's move is a fantastic stretch for upper and lower body. Just click the Fitness Move of the Week on your video screen (1 minute), use the QR code, or go to danielplan.com/fitnessmove.

Praying
Together

Because everything we do in our journey toward health depends on God's power, we end each meeting with prayer and encourage group members to pray for each other during the week.

"If any of you lacks wisdom, you should ask God, who gives generously to all without finding fault, and it will be given to you."
James 1:5

This week, gather in smaller groups of two or three people. Share things that can trigger cravings for you, like getting hungry with no healthy food available or feeling sad with no one to talk to. Also, share the Next Steps you want to take this week, along with any prayer requests related to the 40-day core meal plan or following The Daniel Plan more generally. Then pray for each other in these specific areas. Pray that your partner(s) will be able to follow through on the Next Steps they want to take. Pray for their strategies to resist and even stop cravings. Have someone close with this prayer:

Thank you, Father, that your power is on display in our weakness. Thank you that you are eager to give us the power to overcome our cravings and make healthy choices. We ask you for that power through your Holy Spirit. Please give us wisdom—wisdom to know what to put in our emergency food packs, wisdom to foresee times when we will need to have food on hand, wisdom to discern the difference between when we are truly hungry and when we have some emotional need. Please show us how to nourish ourselves emotionally and physically. Please give us perseverance to stick with our plan. Thank you for your grace that sustains us. I pray this in Jesus' name. Amen.

Designing Your Eating Life

"So I decided there is nothing better than to enjoy food and drink and to find satisfaction in work. Then I realized that these pleasures are from the hand of God. For who can eat or enjoy anything apart from him?"

Ecclesiastes 2:24–25 (NLT)

To make The Daniel Plan work for us over the long haul, we need to give some thought to designing our eating life. How will we handle restaurants and parties? How will we involve family and friends so that food is something to celebrate rather than worry about, causing us to eat in isolation? What does a Daniel Plan kitchen look like? These questions and more will be addressed in this final session.

COMING
TOGETHER

The other members of your group can be a huge source of support in sustaining healthy changes in your life. Before watching the video, check in with each other about your experiences since the last session. For example:

» Briefly share what Next Steps from Session 3 you completed or tried to complete. Were they helpful? If so, how?

» If you did the 10-day detox, what were the results? If you are on the 40-day core meal plan, how is it going? What support do you need?

» Have you been practicing The Daniel Plan in other areas, such as Fitness? If so, what have you done? What is working well for you? What questions do you have? What encouragement do you need?

LEARNING TOGETHER

AN INTERVIEW WITH **Dr. Mark Hyman**

Play the video segment for Session 4. As you watch, use the outline provided to follow along or to take additional notes on anything that stands out to you.

» You'll need basic cooking utensils to set up a Daniel Plan kitchen. To get started, you simply need a pot, a frying pan, a ladle, a stirring spoon, a knife, and a cutting board. For more details, see the items listed in *The Daniel Plan Cookbook*, pages 18 – 21.

» You can speed up prep time during the week if you can take an hour on Sunday night for prep. Hard-boil twelve eggs. Grill some chicken. Chop all your veggies for the week's lunches and dinners. Make some dips. Cook some quinoa or brown rice. Then prep time when you come home in the weekday evenings will be quick.

» Keep the ingredients for a smoothie ready to go in Tupperware containers along with your blender so that the smoothie is quick to prepare.

» Keep on hand healthy foods that last a long time, such as nuts and nut butters, root vegetables, frozen chicken breasts, frozen fish, grains like brown rice, some cans of wild salmon, and a can of sardines.

» Make sure you're never without a ripe avocado in the refrigerator and some salad greens.

» Make your kitchen an inviting place for family and friends. Get some new placemats, good lighting, and a bowl of fresh fruit for decoration. Cook while you spend time with people, giving them tasks like chopping onions or setting the table.

» Involve your children in the cooking so that they learn to do it.

» Which grocery stores have the foods that serve you? Where in the store do they stock the things you need to support you? What are the good brands? Be intentional and willing to learn.

» When you go to the grocery store, think, "What do I need for my house? What do I need for my purse or my bag? What do I need for my workplace? What do I need for my food emergency pack?"

» Shop the perimeter (outside edges) of the store, where the fruits, vegetables, chicken, meat, and fish are. Most of what is in the inner aisles is processed food. However, canned foods (tomatoes, garbanzo beans, salmon) and dried legumes (lentils, peas, beans) are on inner aisles, and those are good for you.

» Find the restaurants near you that serve clean, simple food – nothing fried, no fast food. Ask for substitutions: no bread, double the vegetables instead of potatoes, oil and vinegar for salad dressing.

» If you are going somewhere to eat and you don't know what they serve, fill your pockets or purse with things that are good for you, so you can skip the things that aren't.

- Enlist friends at work to join you in healthy eating. Take turns bringing lunch or snacks for everyone, or bring your own and spend the time together enjoying each other.

- Be an influence on those around you. Create contagious health.

- The Daniel Plan is really about being able to engage in life to the fullest, to be able to love better, to be able to connect with your community, to be able to serve God, to have the best life you can have.

GROWING TOGETHER

Discuss what you learned from the video. Don't feel obliged to answer every question. Select those that most resonate with your group.

1. What did you hear in the video that had the most impact on you?

2. What can you do to your kitchen to make it a more inviting place?

3. Do you have the necessary cooking utensils? Target and Wal-Mart have almost everything you need. Bed, Bath, and Beyond is another good source. What help would make this easier? How can you encourage each other in this area?

Which grocery stores have you found to be the best sources of healthy foods? Have you learned anything about brands (of nut butters, natural mayonnaise, etc.) that would be helpful for others in your group to know?

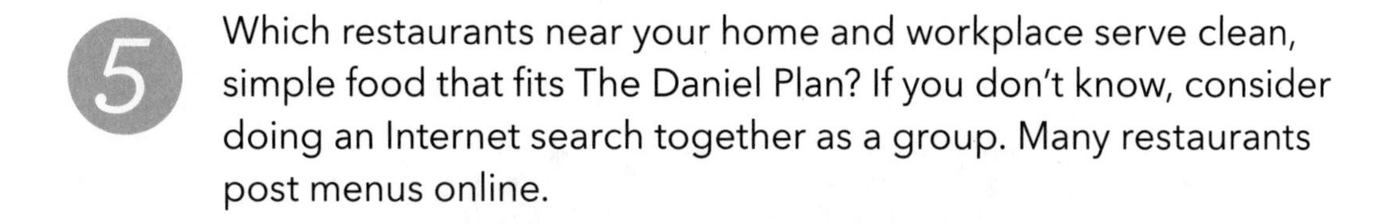

"People should eat and drink and enjoy the fruits of their labor, for these are gifts from God."

Ecclesiastes 3:13 (NLT)

5

Which restaurants near your home and workplace serve clean, simple food that fits The Daniel Plan? If you don't know, consider doing an Internet search together as a group. Many restaurants post menus online.

6

How could you enlist people at your workplace in healthy eating? Is there even one person who could be your ally there?

What is the single biggest challenge you face in designing your eating life? How can the group help you address it?

What have been the top two or three things you have gained from these four sessions on Food? What are you grateful for?

"For the happy heart, life is a continual feast."
Proverbs 15:15 (NLT)

What I Want
to Remember

Complete this activity on your own.

» Briefly review the video outline and any notes you took. Review also any notes from the discussion.

» In the space below, write down the most significant thing you gained from this session—from the video or the discussion. You can share it with the group if you wish.

BETTER TOGETHER

Now that you've talked about some great ideas, let's get practical – and put what you're learning into action. Begin by identifying one or two steps you can take to live what you learned in this session. Then check out the Food Tip of the Week and the Fitness Move of the Week for some fresh ideas to enrich your journey toward health in those areas. Use or adapt whatever is helpful to you!

FOOD

Next Steps

Here are a few suggested activities to help you move forward with designing your eating life. Check one or two boxes next to the options you'd like to try this week – choose what works for you.

- ☐ If you are low on kitchen utensils, consider shopping with a buddy from your group. Use pages 18–21 from *The Daniel Plan Cookbook* as a checklist.

- ☐ Online or in person, study the menus of local restaurants and identify those that serve healthy options. What substitutions could you ask for to make the meals even healthier?

- ☐ Give your kitchen a makeover. Put out flowers or a bowl of fresh fruit. Consider bringing music into the kitchen. How can you make it an inviting place where your family wants to gather to share a meal?

- ☐ If someone in your group is a more experienced cook than you are, request a few lessons. For example, ask them to walk you through making some of the recipes in the 40-day core meal plan. If you are the experienced cook in the group, offer to give some lessons.

- ☐ Involve your children in helping you prepare a meal from the 40-day core meal plan. If they are old enough to learn to use knives, for example, watch a YouTube video together and then give them the veggies to chop. Or have them measure the wet and dry ingredients. Teach them to read the whole recipe, right to the end, before they start the first step, because sometimes something later in the recipe is important to know in the beginning. Make a house rule: if they help to cook the meal, they don't have to help wash the dishes!

- ☐ Find one person at your workplace, school, or neighborhood who is willing to join with you in healthy eating. It may be someone who already eats healthy food, or it may be someone who wants to give it a try. Share with that person what you've learned from The Daniel Plan, and see if he or she would like to have lunch with you once a week, possibly taking turns bringing food to share.

- ☐ Search YouTube for videos that teach knife skills, sautéing, food processing, roasting, or any other cooking skill you want to learn. Even a general search for "cooking skills" yields lots of results.

Food Tip
of the Week

As you're clearing out your pantry and refrigerator, getting rid of unhealthy foods, this week's food tip explains healthy alternatives that you can stock instead. Just click the Food Tip of the Week on your video screen (3 minutes), scan the QR code, or go to danielplan.com/foodtip.

Fitness Move
of the Week

This week's move will show you how to strengthen your upper back muscles so that your shoulders don't round forward. Just click the Fitness Move of the Week on your video screen (1 minute), use the QR code, or go to danielplan.com/fitnessmove.

Praying
Together

Because everything we do in our journey toward health depends on God's power, we end each meeting with prayer and encourage group members to pray for each other during the week.

This week, offer up one- and two-sentence prayers of thanksgiving for what God is doing in your lives. Thank him for what you have learned about healthy eating and for giving you the strength to take the steps you've taken. Thank him for what this group has meant to you.

Have someone close with this prayer:

Thank you, Lord, for the abundance of foods you have given us to eat. Thank you that your desire for us is abundance, not deprivation. Thank you for beginning the transformation of our palates so that we can enjoy the real foods you have made. You created us to take pleasure in real food, and we long to be able to do that more and more. Thank you for the encouragement we have gotten from this group to take the steps we've taken. The power to change comes from you, not from us, so we look to you and ask for your grace to become more and more able to eat and drink to your glory. We want every change we make to honor you, and to give us the energy to do the things you have designed us for. I pray this in Jesus' name. Amen.

Appendix

5-Day Meal Plan

Chapter 10 of *The Daniel Plan* book contains a 40-day core meal plan with recipes to launch you into The Daniel Plan way of eating. The first five days of the plan are reproduced here to give you a sample. Why not try these five days and see how you can experience abundance in this way of eating?

Based on real, whole ingredients, the 40-day meal plan offers meals with a balanced proportion of nutrients to balance blood sugar, hormone levels, and mood, and also to promote cardiovascular health. Eating frequent, clean, small meals throughout the day will not only help you stay energized, but it will also supercharge your metabolism. This way of eating is the most effective way to lose fat and maintain muscle mass. You will feel satisfied and not overstuffed.

The shopping list and recipes follow.

40-DAY CORE MEAL PLAN

Meals that require a recipe are in **bold**; you will find the recipes on pages 304 – 331 of *The Daniel Plan*.

	DAY 1	DAY 2	DAY 3	DAY 4	DAY 5
BREAKFAST	**Strawberry coco choco shake**	Breakfast muffin: 1 scrambled egg, 2 slices baked nitrate-free turkey bacon or avocado on whole grain or sprouted grain English muffin	**Blueberry, spinach, & flax smoothie**	1 c. rolled or steel-cut oatmeal with ½ c. almond milk & ½ c. mixed strawberries and bananas	Breakfast wrap: 1 scrambled egg with ¼ avocado, sliced tomato, basil wrapped in whole grain tortilla
SNACK	⅓ c. **artichoke hummus** with mixed veggie sticks (celery, carrots, cucumber, jicama)	Small apple plus 25 raw almonds	**1 no-bake power bite**	2 tbsp. **crunchy chickpeas** with 1 oz. hard cheese	Small pear or apple with 1 tablespoon almond butter
LUNCH	½ c. quinoa with steamed broccoli, carrots, cauliflower, & **antioxidant dressing**	Low-sodium, nitrate-free turkey breast wrap with tomato, lettuce, 2 tbsp. **artichoke hummus**	**Veggie lentil & chicken sausage soup**	**Citrus salmon skewers** with **supergreens watermelon salad**	**Citrus chicken** as a wrap with 2 tbsp. **artichoke hummus,** romaine, & ¼ avocado
SNACK	2 tbsp. **crunchy chickpeas** with 1 mozzarella cheese stick	1 piece low-glycemic fruit plus 25 raw almonds	**Baba ganoush dip** with mixed veggie sticks (celery, carrots, cucumber, jicama)	**1 no-bake power bite**	**Strawberry coco choco shake**
DINNER	Open-faced ground beef or turkey burger on ½ whole grain English muffin or bun with spinach, tomato, & 1 tbsp. avocado	**Citrus chicken skewers** with brown rice & **supergreens watermelon salad**	**Citrus salmon** filet with grilled/baked asparagus and quinoa	**Grilled Mediterranean lamb kofta** and mixed greens salad	**Veggie lentil & chicken sausage soup** with side of quinoa or brown rice
HEALTHY TREAT	1 piece of fruit chopped and sprinkled with cinnamon	**Dark chocolate avocado mousse cup**	**Grapefruit and pomegranate salad with coconut**	**Chocolate and walnut dipped frozen banana pops**	Chopped fruit salad

Shopping List

Get stocked for success! You can add or modify as needed. Feel free to swap out fruits and vegetables based on the season or your tastes.

Important notes:

1. Compare your shopping list to what's already in your pantry before you go shopping.
2. If the specific size of an item is not listed, you can buy the smallest version.
3. Suggested quantities are based on the recipe serving sizes. Entrees generally serve 4; snacks generally serve 1–2.

FRESH PRODUCE

- ☐ 4 apples
- ☐ 2 avocados
- ☐ 4 bananas
- ☐ 1 large container blueberries
- ☐ 4 lemons
- ☐ 2 limes
- ☐ 1 orange
- ☐ 1 pink grapefruit
- ☐ 1 pomegranate
- ☐ 1 large container strawberries
- ☐ Small watermelon or other melon
- ☐ 1 package arugula
- ☐ 1 bunch asparagus
- ☐ 2 bags (8–9 oz.) of fresh baby spinach, or one small bunch
- ☐ 2 red bell peppers
- ☐ 1 head broccoli
- ☐ 2 heads purple or green cabbage
- ☐ 1 bag carrots
- ☐ 1 bag celery
- ☐ 1 eggplant
- ☐ 1 bulb garlic
- ☐ 1 jicama
- ☐ 2 packages or heads of kale
- ☐ 2 medium onions
- ☐ 1 bunch parsley
- ☐ 2 medium red-skinned or purple potatoes or 1 turnip
- ☐ 1 head romaine lettuce
- ☐ 1 small bag snow peas or green beans

BAKERY/BREADS

- ☐ 1 package taco-sized sprouted or whole grain tortillas
- ☐ 1 package sprouted whole grain muffins

MEAT/FISH

- ☐ 2 pounds chicken breasts or cutlets
- ☐ 6 chicken sausages
- ☐ 1 pound lean ground turkey or beef
- ☐ 1 pound sliced turkey breast, nitrate-free
- ☐ 2 pounds wild salmon
- ☐ 1 pound ground lamb

EGGS & DAIRY

- ☐ 1 dozen cage-free or organic eggs
- ☐ 1 small package feta cheese
- ☐ 1 large container nonfat plain Greek yogurt
- ☐ 1 package hard, unprocessed cheese

PASTA, GRAINS, LEGUMES

- ☐ 1 package brown rice (preferably jasmine) or black rice
- ☐ 1 pound gluten-free pasta (e.g., brown rice pasta)
- ☐ 1 pound lentils
- ☐ 1 container old-fashioned rolled oats
- ☐ 1 package quinoa

FREEZER SECTION

- ☐ 1 package mixed frozen berries
- ☐ 1 package frozen strawberries

CANNED FOODS

- ☐ 1 jar unsweetened applesauce
- ☐ 1 can artichokes in water
- ☐ 1 15-oz. can cannellini, great northern, or black beans
- ☐ 3 cans garbanzo beans/chickpeas
- ☐ 2 qts. low-sodium chicken or vegetable broth
- ☐ 1 jar kalamata or black olives
- ☐ 2 containers fresh salsa or your favorite recipe
- ☐ 1 can chopped tomatoes
- ☐ 1 15-oz. can organic tomato sauce

CONDIMENTS/SAUCES

- ☐ 1 bottle unfiltered apple cider vinegar
- ☐ 1 bottle balsamic or red wine vinegar
- ☐ 1 container coconut oil or grape seed oil
- ☐ 1 bottle Dijon mustard
- ☐ 1 bottle extra-virgin olive oil (or cooking spray)
- ☐ 1 jar raw honey
- ☐ 1 small bottle low-sodium soy sauce or tamari
- ☐ 1 small bottle sesame oil
- ☐ 1 small bottle sesame tahini paste
- ☐ 1 small bag stevia
- ☐ 1 can tomato paste
- ☐ 1 jar organic or vegan mayonnaise

NUTS/SEEDS

- ☐ 1 box unsweetened coconut milk or almond milk
- ☐ 1 box unsweetened almond milk
- ☐ 1 jar almond or other nut butter
- ☐ 1 bag almond meal/flour
- ☐ 1 bag raw almonds
- ☐ 1 bag slivered almonds
- ☐ 1 package chia seeds
- ☐ 1 package ground flax meal
- ☐ 1 bag unsalted sunflower seeds
- ☐ 1 bag raw walnuts

MISCELLANEOUS

- ☐ 1 container chocolate flavor plant-based protein powder (optional)
- ☐ 70% cocoa chocolate chips/bar
- ☐ 1 container quality plant-based protein powder

SPICES/HERBS

- ☐ Black pepper
- ☐ Cayenne pepper
- ☐ Chili powder
- ☐ Cumin
- ☐ Curry powder
- ☐ Dill
- ☐ Dried mustard
- ☐ Dry oregano
- ☐ Garlic powder
- ☐ Kosher or sea salt
- ☐ Onion powder
- ☐ Vanilla extract

Recipes

D ***indicates detox-compatible recipes***

ANTIOXIDANT SALAD DRESSING D

¼ cup raw unfiltered apple cider vinegar

2 tablespoons extra-virgin olive, grape seed, or coconut oil

1 clove garlic, crushed

2 tablespoons lemon juice, plus 1 teaspoon grated zest

1 teaspoon ground flax seed

1 teaspoon dry mustard

½ teaspoon oregano

Ground black pepper and salt to taste

Briskly whisk together vinegar and oil until mixed well (or you can put them in a closed container and shake vigorously). Add remaining ingredients, and whisk (or shake) together until well incorporated. You can vary this dressing to suit your taste by adding other herbs and spices such as basil, tarragon, rosemary, and dill. ***Serves 3–4***

ARTICHOKE HUMMUS D

1 (15-ounce) can chickpeas/garbanzo beans

1 cup artichoke hearts, drained and chopped

2 cloves fresh garlic, crushed

2 tablespoons lemon juice

1 tablespoon olive oil

1 tablespoon water

1 tablespoon sesame tahini

Ground black pepper and salt to taste

Combine all ingredients in a food processor and pulse until smooth. Transfer to a bowl. Chill and serve with mixed veggie sticks such as celery, jicama, and carrots.

Serves 8 (⅓ cup each)

BABA GANOUSH DIP Ⓓ

1 large eggplant
¼ cup tahini, plus more as needed
3 garlic cloves, minced
¼ cup fresh lemon juice, plus more as needed
1 pinch ground cumin
1 pinch salt
1 tablespoon chopped fresh flat-leaf parsley

Preheat oven to 375°. Prick the eggplant with a fork in several places and place on a baking sheet. Bake until very soft, about 20 to 30 minutes. Remove from the oven, let cool slightly. Peel off and discard the skin. Place the eggplant flesh in a bowl. Using a fork, mash the eggplant well. Add the tahini, garlic, lemon juice, and cumin, and mix well. Season with salt, then taste and add more tahini and/or lemon juice, if needed. Transfer the mixture to a serving bowl. Sprinkle parsley over the top. Serve at room temperature. ***Serves 4 (¼ cup each)***

BLUEBERRY, SPINACH, AND FLAX SMOOTHIE Ⓓ

2 cups unsweetened almond or coconut milk
2 tablespoons ground flax seeds
1 scoop unsweetened protein powder
1 cup spinach
½ cup fresh or frozen blueberries
½ cup crushed ice

Process first five ingredients in a blender. Add ice and process until smooth. ***Serves 2***

CHOCOLATE AND WALNUT DIPPED FROZEN BANANA POPS

8 ounces of 70% or higher dark chocolate,
broken into pieces or chunks
2 bananas, cut in half
2 tablespoons crushed walnuts
4 wooden skewers or popsicle sticks

Melt chocolate in a double boiler or microwave. If using a microwave, be careful not to "cook" the chocolate; nuke it for 30 seconds at a time until soft and gooey. Let chocolate sit for about 5 minutes to cool slightly. Place crushed walnuts on a plate. Thread banana onto skewer or popsicle stick. Dip half of banana into melted chocolate and roll carefully into crushed walnuts. Repeat until all banana pieces are dipped. Place dipped bananas onto a tray lined with wax paper, and freeze for at least 4 hours, preferably overnight.

Serves 4

CITRUS MARINADE FOR CHICKEN OR SALMON SKEWERS/VEGGIES

1 lemon, juiced plus 1 teaspoon zest
2 limes, juiced plus 1 teaspoon zest
1 tablespoon balsamic vinegar
2 teaspoons olive oil
Ground black pepper and salt
2 pounds of chicken, salmon, or veggies, cut into 2-inch pieces

Whisk together first five ingredients until well incorporated. Place chicken, salmon, or veggies separately in marinade. Marinate for at least 1 hour, up to overnight for the chicken or veggies, before cooking. Thread chicken or salmon and veggies onto skewers and grill or bake until thoroughly cooked. This will make enough for one lunch and one dinner for two people. Make one batch with chicken and one with fish for Days 1-5.

Serves 4–5

CRUNCHY CHICKPEAS D

4 cups garbanzo beans, drained and rinsed
2 teaspoons extra-virgin olive oil
1 teaspoon ground cumin
1 teaspoon ground chili powder
½ teaspoon cayenne pepper

Preheat oven to 400°, and arrange a rack in the middle. Place the chickpeas in a large bowl and toss with the remaining ingredients until evenly coated. Spread the chickpeas in an even layer on a rimmed baking sheet and bake until crisp, about 30 to 40 minutes.

Serves 12 (1 ounce each)

DARK CHOCOLATE AVOCADO MOUSSE CUP

⅔ cup of 70% or higher dark chocolate, chopped

1 tablespoon coconut oil

1 teaspoon stevia extract

1 tablespoon brewed coffee

½ teaspoon pure vanilla extract

1 avocado

TOPPING: ***½ cup whole strawberries or toasted almonds (optional).***

Melt chocolate in a double boiler or microwave. If using a microwave, be careful not to "cook" the chocolate; nuke it for 30 seconds at a time until soft and gooey. Add coconut oil, sweetener, coffee, and vanilla extract to melted chocolate, and mix well. Scoop out avocado and blend it into the chocolate mixture. You can use a hand or stick blender to achieve a smooth consistency. Scoop out into 4 equal portions and chill for at least 2 hours. Top with a spoon of toasted almonds or strawberries before serving. ***Serves 4***

GRAPEFRUIT AND POMEGRANATE SALAD WITH COCONUT

1 medium pink grapefruit

½ cup pomegranate seeds

Juice of 1 orange

1 tablespoon shredded unsweetened coconut

Peel grapefruit and cut it into bite sizes. Remove pomegranate seeds from pomegranate. (You can also buy pomegranate seeds ready to use.) In a mixing bowl combine grapefruit, pomegranate, and coconut. Add the juice of one orange. Mix well. Serve cold. ***Serves 2***

GRILLED MEDITERRANEAN LAMB KOFTA D

3 cloves garlic, crushed

2 tablespoons onion, grated

¼ cup fresh parsley, chopped

1 teaspoon salt

2 teaspoons ground black pepper

1 teaspoon allspice

1 teaspoon paprika

1 tablespoon ground coriander

1 pound ground lamb

Wooden or metal skewers

Preheat grill to medium heat. (You can also forgo the skewers and shape lamb into sausages and cook over medium heat in a sauté pan.) In a large bowl, combine crushed garlic, spices, and seasonings and, working with hands, incorporate into ground lamb until well blended.

Form seasoned lamb mixture into a sausage-like shape around skewers. If using wooden skewers, make sure to soak the skewers in water for at least 30 minutes before placing on grill. Cook kofta skewers on the preheated grill, turning occasionally, for about 7-8 minutes or until desired doneness. ***Serves 3–4***

NO-BAKE POWER BITES

1 cup rolled oats

½ cup unsweetened shredded coconut plus ⅓ cup for topping

1 scoop chocolate protein powder

2 tablespoons natural almond or other nut butter

½ cup ground flax meal

½ cup dark chocolate chips (70% or more cocoa powder)

1 teaspoon stevia extract

⅔ cup unsweetened coconut milk

1 teaspoon pure vanilla extract

In a small bowl, mix all ingredients thoroughly. Chill in the refrigerator for an hour. Roll into 2-inch balls, then roll in shredded coconut. Set balls on wax paper in an airtight container in the refrigerator or freezer.

Allow to rest at room temperature for 5 minutes before eating. ***Serves 20–25 (1 ball each)***

STRAWBERRY COCO CHOCO SHAKE

1 cup frozen strawberries

1 cup unsweetened coconut milk

1 scoop chocolate protein powder

1 tablespoon ground flax seed

1 scoop ice

Combine ingredients in a blender. Add ice and blend until smooth. Serve cold. ***Serves 1***

SUPER GREENS WATERMELON SALAD

2 cups arugula
2 cups kale, chopped
2 cups spinach
1 cup watermelon, diced (or grapefruit)
1 tablespoon toasted unsalted sunflower seeds
Antioxidant salad dressing (see recipe, p. 82 of this guide)

Chop kale to bite-size pieces. (Tip: Stack kale leaves into a pile. Roll the leaves together. Run a sharp knife through roll of kale to create thin to medium strips.) Chop watermelon into cubes. Mix arugula, spinach, and kale together. Add watermelon cubes to salad. Drizzle with 2 tablespoons of homemade salad dressing. Top with toasted sunflower seeds. *Serves 2*

VEGGIE, LENTIL, AND CHICKEN SAUSAGE SOUP D

1 pound lentils, raw
4 links chicken sausage
1 tablespoon olive oil
1 cup onion, chopped
½ cup carrot, chopped
½ cup celery, chopped
1 teaspoon salt
1 teaspoon ground black pepper
¼ teaspoon cayenne pepper
½ teaspoon ground cumin
1 cup canned tomatoes, no salt added
2 quarts organic low-sodium chicken broth

Heat olive oil in a large soup pot over medium heat. Add onion, carrot, celery, and salt and sweat until the onions are translucent, approximately 5 minutes. Add the lentils, tomatoes, broth, peppers, and cumin. Stir to combine. Increase the heat to high and bring just to a boil. Reduce the heat to low, cover, and cook at a low simmer until the lentils are tender, approximately 35 to 40 minutes. Using a sharp knife make a cut on one end of the sausage links. Remove sausage meat from link casing by squeezing meat through the cut on the link. Heat olive oil in a large pan over medium heat. Add sausage meat and cook until golden brown, breaking up the meat as you cook it. Drain any excess fat. Add to finished lentil soup and serve hot. *Serves 6*

Cleaning Out Your Pantry

FOODS AND INGREDIENTS TO AVOID

white flour	white sugar	high-fructose corn syrup (HFCS)
white rice	juice	monosodium glutamate (MSG)
regular sodas	diet sodas	sports drinks and other sweetened beverages
phosphoric acid	soy protein isolate	sodium and calcium caseinate
sulfites	carrageenan	nitrites and nitrates
artificial flavors	artificial sweeteners (except stevia)	artificial colors and dyes
trans fats–partially hydrogenated and hydrogenated fats		

EASY REPLACEMENTS AND ALTERNATIVES

Replace This	With This
mass market vegetable oil	unrefined, cold-pressed, and expeller-pressed oils such as extra-virgin olive oil, grape seed oil, coconut oil, avocado oil, and sesame oil
shortening	coconut butter or oil

Replace This	With This
white flour	whole grain wheat flour, organic sprouted grain, almond flour, gluten-free flour, or organic cornmeal
sugary cereals	old-fashioned oats, steel-cut oats, buckwheat, or kasha
milk or cream (for lactose intolerant)	unsweetened coconut or almond milk
fried potato or corn chips	baked corn, baked vegetable, or brown rice chips
cream-based soups	creamy bean-based soups, vegetable puree soups, and soups made with alternative healthy milks
white pasta	whole wheat pasta, brown rice pasta, or quinoa pasta
white rice	brown or black rice, quinoa, barley
table salt	kosher or sea salt
white sugar	raw honey, pure maple syrup, whole stevia extract*
sugary snacks	nuts, nut butters, dark chocolate, plain Greek yogurt with berries or a little honey
gummy candies	dried fruits (figs, dates, etc.)
condiments and sauces with MSG or HFCS	naturally produced products with no added sugar, spices, vinegars, herbs
chip dips	guacamole, hummus, tzatziki, salsa
fruit juice	herbal teas, water with citrus wedges

* For baking, sugar alternatives do not react the same, so an equal swap may not work. *The Daniel Plan Cookbook* and the danielplan.com website offer excellent dessert recipes that use sugar alternatives appropriately.

Top 10 Tips to Curb Your Cravings

1. **Avoid your triggers:** The reality is that you crave what you eat, so as you make healthier choices, your old cravings will weaken. Certain situations can sabotage your weight loss efforts. For example, going to the movies can ignite your brain's emotional memory centers and make you feel like you need an extra-large tub of popcorn. Identify the people, places, and things that trigger your cravings and plan ahead to avoid making an unhealthy choice. For example, take a healthy snack to the movies so you are not tempted to buy popcorn. This will save you money too!

2. **Balance your blood sugar:** Research studies indicate that low blood sugar levels are associated with lower overall blood flow to the brain, which can jeopardize your ability to make good decisions. To keep your blood sugar stable, eat a nutritious breakfast with protein, such as eggs, a protein shake, or nut butters. Plan to eat smaller, more frequent meals throughout the day. Also, avoid eating two to three hours before bedtime.

3. **Eliminate sugar, artificial sweeteners, and refined carbs:** It's best to go cold turkey. Eliminate refined sugars, sodas, fruit juices, and artificial sweeteners from your diet, as these can trigger cravings. Many doctors believe that sugar is the primary cause of obesity, high blood pressure, heart disease, and diabetes. The latest statistics reveal that the average American consumes 130 pounds of sugar a year!

4. **Eat SLOW carb, not LOW carb:** Eat carbohydrates that don't spike your blood sugar. Choose high fiber carbs that keep you fuller longer and help reduce your sugar cravings. You can increase your fiber intake by eating vegetables, fruits, beans, and whole grains. Fiber will assist weight loss because it fills up your stomach and helps you

moderate your portions. Carbohydrates are essential to good health and are not the enemy. Bad carbohydrates such as simple sugars and refined products are the ones to avoid.

5. **Drink more water:** Sometimes hunger is disguised as dehydration. When you are dehydrated, your body will increase your hunger level in an attempt to get more water to rehydrate. Try drinking a glass of water before your meals to make you feel fuller and thus moderate your food intake.

6. **Make protein 25 percent of your diet:** Protein fills you up and keeps you satisfied longer. It also regulates your blood sugar and makes your body release appetite-suppressing hormones.

7. **Manage your stress:** Stress triggers hormones that activate cravings. Chronic stress has been associated with obesity, addiction, anxiety, depression, Alzheimer's disease, heart disease, and cancer. Adopt a daily stress management program that includes deep breathing exercises, prayer, and other relaxation techniques.

8. **Follow the 90/10 Rule:** Give yourself a break. Make great food choices 90 percent of the time, and allow yourself margin to enjoy some of your favorite foods on occasion. This way you won't feel deprived, and you will avoid bingeing on something you'll regret later.

9. **Get moving:** Research shows that physical activity can curb cravings. Plan out your exercise for the week and schedule it on your calendar. Make the commitment to yourself just like any other important meeting or appointment.

10. **Get seven to eight hours of sleep a night:** Sleep deprivation can increase cravings. Check out our tips for healthy sleep habits on danielplan.com.

Group Guidelines

Our goal: To provide a safe environment where participants experience authentic community and spiritual growth.

OUR VALUES	
Group Attendance	To give priority to the group meeting. We will call or email if we will be late or absent.
Safe Environment	To help create a safe place where people can be heard and feel loved.
Respect Differences	To be gentle and gracious to people with different spiritual maturity, personal opinions, or personalities. Remember we are all works in progress!
Confidentiality	To keep anything that is shared strictly confidential and within the group, and to avoid sharing information about those outside the group.
Encouragement for Growth	We want to spiritually multiply our life by serving others with our God-given gifts.
Rotating Hosts/Leaders and Homes	To encourage different people to host the group in their homes, and to rotate the responsibility of facilitating each meeting.

We have found that groups thrive when they talk about expectations up front and come into agreement on some of the following details.

Refreshments/mealtimes ______________________________

Child care ______________________________

When we will meet (day of week) ______________________________

Where we will meet (place) ______________________________

We will begin at (time) ______________ and end at ______________

We will look for a compatible time to attend a worship service together.

Our primary worship service time will be ______________________

Leadership 101

Congratulations! You have responded to the call to help shepherd Jesus' flock. There are few other tasks in the family of God that surpass the contribution you will be making. As you prepare to lead, whether it is one session or four, here are a few thoughts to keep in mind. We encourage you to read these and review them with each new discussion leader before he or she leads.

1. **Remember that you are not alone.** God knows everything about you, and he knew that you would be asked to lead your group. It is common for leaders to feel that they are not ready to lead. Moses, Solomon, Jeremiah, Timothy—they all were reluctant to lead. God promises, "Never will I leave you; never will I forsake you" (Hebrews 13:5). You will be blessed as you serve.

2. **Don't try to do it alone.** Pray right now for God to help you build a healthy leadership team. If you can enlist a co-leader to help you lead the group, you will find your experience to be much richer. That person might take half the group in a second discussion circle if your group is as large as ten people or more. Your co-leader might lead the prayer time or handle the hosting tasks, welcoming people and getting them refreshments. This is your chance to involve as many people as you can in building a healthy group. All you have to do is call and ask people to help; you'll be surprised at the response.

3. **Just be yourself.** God wants you to use your unique gifts and temperament. Don't try to do things exactly like another leader; do them in a way that fits you! Just admit it when you don't have an answer, and apologize when you make a mistake. Your group will love you for it, and you'll sleep better at night.

4. **Prepare for your meeting ahead of time.** Review the session, view the video, and write down your responses to each question. If paper and pens are needed, such as for gathering group members' names and email addresses (see "Coming Together" in Session 1), be sure you have the necessary supplies. Think about which "Next Steps" you will do.

   If you're leading Session 1, look over the Group Guidelines and be ready to review them with the group. If child care will be an issue for your group, for example, be prepared to talk about options. Some groups have the adults share the cost of a babysitter (or two) to care for children in a different part of the house where the adults are meeting. Other groups use one home for the kids and another for the adults. A third idea is to rotate the responsibility of caring for the children in the same home or one nearby.

5. **Pray for your group members by name.** Before you begin your session, go around the room in your mind and pray for each member. You may want to review the group's prayer list at least once a week. Ask God to use your time together to work in the heart of each person uniquely. Expect God to lead you to whomever he wants you to encourage or challenge in a special way.

6. **When you ask a question, be patient.** Read each question aloud and wait for someone to respond. Sometimes people need a moment or two of silence to think about the question, and if silence doesn't bother you, it won't bother anyone else. After someone responds, affirm the response with a simple "thanks" or "good job." Then ask, "How about somebody else?" or "Would someone who hasn't shared like to add anything?" Be sensitive to new people or reluctant members who aren't ready to participate yet. If you give them a safe setting, they will open up over time. Don't go around the circle and have everyone answer every question. Your goal is a conversation in which the group members talk to each other in a natural way.

7. **Break up into small groups each week or people won't stay.** If your group has more than eight people, we strongly encourage you to have the group gather sometimes in discussion circles of three or four people during the "Growing Together" section of the study. With a greater opportunity to talk in a small circle, people will connect more with the study, apply more quickly what they are learning, and ultimately get more out of it. A small circle also encourages a quiet person to participate and tends to minimize the effect of a more vocal or dominant member. It can also help people feel more loved in your group. When you gather again at the end of the section, you can have one person summarize the highlights from each circle.

   Small circles are also helpful during prayer time. People who are not accustomed to praying aloud will feel more comfortable trying it with just two or three others. Also, prayer requests won't take as much time, so circles will have more time to actually pray. When you gather back with the whole group, you can have one person from each circle briefly update everyone on the prayer requests.

8. **One final challenge for new leaders:** Before your opportunity to lead, look up each of the four passages listed below. Read each one as a devotional exercise to help equip you with a shepherd's heart. If you do this, you will be more than ready for your first meeting.

   Matthew 9:36
   1 Peter 5:2–4
   Psalm 23
   Ezekiel 34:11–16

For additional tips and resources, go to danielplan.com/tools.

Memory Verses

SESSION 1

"Do you not know that your bodies are temples of the Holy Spirit, who is in you, whom you have received from God? You are not your own; you were bought at a price. Therefore honor God with your bodies."

1 Corinthians 6:19–20

SESSION 2

"So whether you eat or drink, or whatever you do, do it all for the glory of God."

1 Corinthians 10:31 (NLT)

SESSION 3

"Each time [God] said, 'My grace is all you need. My power works best in weakness.' So now I am glad to boast about my weaknesses, so that the power of Christ can work through me."

2 Corinthians 12:9 (NLT)

SESSION 4

"People should eat and drink and enjoy the fruits of their labor, for these are gifts from God."

Ecclesiastes 3:13 (NLT)

About the Contributors

GUEST SPEAKERS

Mark Hyman, MD is the Director of the Cleveland Clinic for Functional Medicine, chairman of the Institute for Functional Medicine, and founder and medical director of The UltraWellness Center. He is the #1 *New York Times* bestselling author of *The Blood Sugar Solution 10-Day Detox Diet, The 10-Day Detox Cookbook, The Blood Sugar Solution, The Blood Sugar Solution Cookbook, UltraMetabolism, The UltraMind Solution,* and *The Ultrasimple Diet,* and coauthor of *The Daniel Plan* and *UltraPrevention.*

Dee Eastman is the Founding Director of The Daniel Plan that has helped over 15,000 people lose 260,000 pounds in the first year alone. Dee completed her education in Health Science with an emphasis in long-term lifestyle change. Her experience in corporate wellness and ministry has fueled her passion to help people transform their health while drawing closer to God. She coauthored the *Doing Life Together* Bible study series and was a contributing author of *The Daniel Plan.*

SIGNATURE CHEFS

Sally Cameron is a professional chef, author, recipe developer, educator, certified health coach, and one of the contributors to *The Daniel Plan Cookbook*. Sally's passion is to inspire people to create great-tasting meals at home using healthy ingredients and easy techniques. Sally is the publisher of the popular food blog, *A Food Centric Life*. She holds a culinary degree from The Art Institute and health coaching certification from The Institute for Integrative Nutrition.

Robert Sturm is one of California's premier chefs and food designers. He has been in the food service industry for more than thirty years, working as an independent consultant to leading restaurants chains around the country. He has been featured in many publications, appears on television and radio, and has been a featured chef at the United Nations, the White House, and the Kremlin. Robert is the three-time winner of the U.S. Chef's Open, a past gold medal member of the U.S. Culinary Olympic Team, and has won many national and international culinary titles and food design awards.

Mareya Ibrahim is best known as "The Fit Foodie." She is an award-winning entrepreneur, television chef, author, and one of The Daniel Plan signature chefs. She is also the CEO and founder of Grow Green Industries, Inc. and cocreator of eatCleaner, the premier lifestyle destination for fit food information. Her book *The Clean Eating Handbook* is touted as the "go-to" guide for anyone looking to eat cleaner and get leaner. She is a featured chef on ABC's Emmy-nominated cooking show *Recipe Rehab,* eHow.com, and Livestrong, and the food expert for San Diego's Channel 6 News.

FITNESS TEAM

Sean Foy is an internationally renowned authority on fitness, weight management, and healthy living. As an author, exercise physiologist, behavioral coach, and speaker, Sean has earned the reputation as "America's Fast Fitness Expert." With an upbeat and sensible approach to making fitness happen, he's taken the message of "simple moves" fitness all over the world. Sean is the author of *Fitness That Works, Walking 4 Wellness, The Burst Workout,* and a contributing author *The Daniel Plan.*

Basheerah Ahmad is a well-known celebrity fitness expert, with a heart for serving God's people. Whether it be through television appearances (*Dr. Phil, The Doctors*), writing fitness and nutrition books, speaking publicly about health, or teaching classes in under-served communities, Basheerah has dedicated her life to improving the health of people everywhere. She has a MS in Exercise Science and numerous certifications in fitness and nutrition. She was a lead fitness instructor for *The Daniel Plan in Action* fitness video series.

Tony "The Marine" Lattimore is one of Southern California's premier fitness experts. A skilled personal trainer who privately trains professional athletes, celebrities, and community leaders, he has competed nationally as a bodybuilder. Tony's fitness expertise was featured in P90X and *The Daniel Plan in Action* fitness video series. His powerhouse workouts have a reputation for making fitness fun and exhilarating.

Kevin Forbes has a passion for inspiring others to build healthy habits and push through their physical and mental boundaries. Kevin has helped others grow as a personal trainer, group fitness instructor, and fitness professional. Most recently, he was a featured fitness instructor in *The Daniel Plan in Action* fitness video series. Kevin mentors not only future fitness leaders but also the foster youth in his local community.

Janet Hertogh shares her love and enthusiasm for teaching in the classroom as an elementary school teacher and in a variety of fitness classes at Saddleback Church. Her passion for life change and transformation is a central theme wherever she goes. Her Masters Degree in Education along with her AFAA and personal training certification make her fully equipped to influence many. Janet was a featured fitness instructor in *The Daniel Plan in Action* fitness video series.

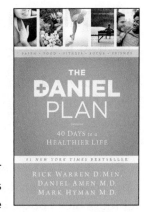

THE DANIEL PLAN

The Daniel Plan Cookbook

Healthy Eating for Life

Rick Warren D. Min., Daniel Amen M.D., and Mark Hyman M.D. featuring The Daniel Plan Signature Chefs

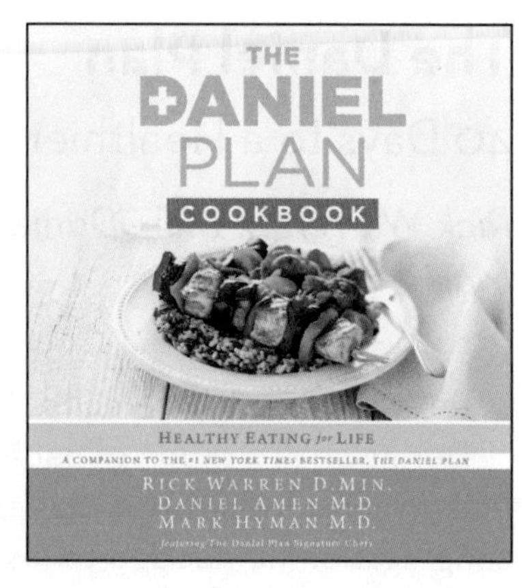

Based on *The Daniel Plan* book, *The Daniel Plan Cookbook: 40 Days to a Healthier Life* is a beautiful four-color cookbook filled with more than 100 delicious, Daniel Plan-approved recipes that offer an abundance of options to bring healthy cooking into your kitchen.

No boring drinks or bland entrées here. Get ready to enjoy appetizing, inviting, clean, simple meals to share in community with your friends and family.

Healthy cooking can be easy and delicious, and *The Daniel Plan Cookbook* is the mouth-watering companion to *The Daniel Plan* book and *The Daniel Plan Journal* to help transform your health in the most head-turning way imaginably—from the inside out.

Available in stores and online!

THE DANIEL PLAN

The Daniel Plan Journal

40 Days to a Healthier Life

Rick Warren and The Daniel Plan Team

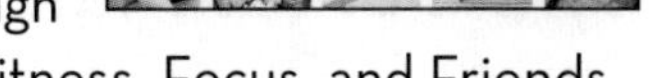

The Perfect Daniel Plan Companion for Better Overall Health

Research shows that tracking your food and exercise greatly contributes to your long-term success. Maximize your momentum by exploring and charting your journey through the five key Essentials of The Daniel Plan — Faith, Food, Fitness, Focus, and Friends.

Taking readers of *The Daniel Plan: 40 Days to a Healthier Life* to the next level, *The Daniel Plan Journal* is the perfect companion, providing encouraging reminders about your health. On the days you need a little boost, *The Daniel Plan Journal* has the daily Scripture, inspiration, and motivation you need to stay on track and keep moving forward.

Available in stores and online!

THE DANIEL PLAN

The Daniel Plan in Action

40 Day Fitness Programs With Dynamic Workouts

Introduction by Rick Warren D. Min.

The Daniel Plan in Action is a 40-day fitness system with an innovative approach to creating a healthy lifestyle, rooted and framed by five life areas: faith, food, fitness, focus and friends. Three expert instructors lead the variety of inspiring workouts with a strong backbone of faith and community, complemented by a soundtrack of exclusive Christian music. This 4-session and 8-session systems focus on an abundance of healthy choices offering you the encouragement and inspiration you need to succeed.

Go to DanielPlan.com now to learn more.

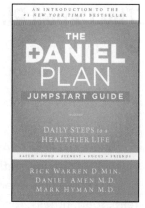